Communications
Close

Global
Networks

Communications Close-up

Global Networks

Ian Graham

First published in paperback in 2003 by
Evans Brothers Limited
2A Portman Mansions
Chiltern Street
London
W1U 6NR

First published in 2000
Printed in Hong Kong

Designer: Simon Borrough
Editor: Nicola Barber
Illustrations: Richard Morris, Hardlines

British Library Cataloguing in
Publication Data

Graham Ian – 1953-
   Global networks – (Communications
close up)
   1. Telecommunication systems – Juvenile
literature
   I. Title
   621.3'82

ISBN 0237526298

Acknowledgements

Cover David Parker/Science Photo Library **page 6** BT
Corporate Picture Library; a BT photograph **page 7**
(top left) Mary Kate Denny/Tony Stone Images
(top right) With thanks to Nokia (bottom right)
Science Museum/Science and Society Picture Library
page 8 and 9 Cable and Wireless Company **page 10**
NASA/Science Photo Library **page 11** (middle left)
Dennis O'Clair/Tony Stone Images (bottom left) Jerry
Kobalenko/Tony Stone Images (bottom right) Adam
Hart-Davis/Science Photo Library **page 13**
Motorola/Science Photo Library **page 15**
NASA/Science Photo Library **page 16** Julian
Baum/Science Photo Library **page 17** (left) David
Parker/Science Photo Library (right) NASA/Science
Photo Library **page 18** (top) Martin Dohrn/Science
Photo Library (bottom left) Dennis O'Clair/Tony Stone
Images **page 19** NASA/Science and Society Picture
Library **page 20** Patrick Barth/Rex Features **page 21**
Keith Kent/Science Photo Library **page 22** Jerry
Mason/Science Photo Library **page 24** Don
Smetzer/Tony Stone Images **page 25** (top) Philippe
Plailly/Eurelios/Science Photo Library (bottom) FPG
International/Robert Harding Picture Library **page 26**
Screenshot provided courtesy of Activision, Inc. ©
1999 Activision, Inc. **page 27** Sam Ogden/Science
Photo Library **page 28** (top) Geoff
Tompkinson/Science Photo Library (bottom) Pete
Seaward/Tony Stone Images **page 29** Dan Bosler/Tony
Stone Images **page 30** (top) Shaun Egan/Tony Stone
Images **page 31** Alex Bartel/Science Photo Library
page 33 Hulton Getty **page 35** Darryl Torckler/Tony
Stone Images **page 36** Rex Features **page 37** Tony
Buxton/Science Photo Library **page 39** GE Astro
Space/Science Photo Library **page 40** (right)
ESA/Science Photo Library (left) David A.
Hardy/Science Photo Library **page 41** US
Navy/Science Photo Library

CONTENTS

THE TELEPHONE

THANKS TO THE TELEPHONE, TALKING TO SOMEONE IN ANOTHER COUNTRY IS AS EASY AS TALKING TO SOMEONE IN THE NEXT STREET. THE INTERNATIONAL TELEPHONE NETWORK SPANS THE GLOBE LIKE A VAST SPIDER'S WEB AND THERE ARE TELEPHONES EVERYWHERE.

Every telephone is connected to a global telecommunications network of electric wires, fibre optic cables and radio waves. The network is extremely complicated, with millions of interconnections. If one part of the system breaks down, calls can be sent round the fault. Computerised switching centres, or exchanges, control which line each call is sent along to reach its final destination.

MAKING CONNECTIONS

When you make a telephone call, the number you dial allows the network to connect your telephone to the correct telephone at the other end. For calls outside the UK, an internationally agreed code identifies the country you want to contact. Then an area code identifies which part of the country the telephone is in. The final part of the number identifies one particular telephone.

The call starts out travelling along electric wires, but at some point in its journey it is switched on to faster, fibre optic cables. It may fly across the countryside as a microwave radio signal, or snake along a cable lying on the sea bed, or even head out into space to a communications satellite orbiting high above the Earth.

MAKING DIGITAL CALLS

Today, telephone lines are used for a lot more than people's voices. Fax machines send copies of documents as coded streams of tones (sounds) along telephone lines. Computer data, too, is sent as tones through devices called modems. A modem changes the data into tones at one end of the line and back into data again at the other end. However, modems are quite slow (see pages 22-3). An ISDN (Integrated Services Digital Network) line is faster because computer data is sent directly

In a modern telephone exchange, banks of computerised switches route thousands of incoming telephone calls on to the right lines to reach their destinations.

telephones, called Personal Digital Assistants (PDAs), can send faxes and email by radio, too. Satellite telephones communicate by radio via satellites in space. The most advanced mobile telephone is worn on the wrist like a watch. It has no keypad. Instead, the caller dials a number by speaking into the phone, which has a built-in voice recognition system.

You can make a telephone call from almost anywhere, thanks to the mobile phone. Mobiles are linked to the international telephone network by radio.

Although it looks like a mobile phone from the outside, this 'communicator' opens to reveal a computer keyboard and a small screen. Using these features, this telephone can be used to send faxes and emails.

from one end to the other without having to be changed into tones. Even faster connections will be available in the next ten years to carry torrents of digital communications, from digitised voice calls to computer data, and from video pictures to email.

RADIO CALLS

Telephones no longer have to be connected to the network by cable. Cordless phones connect the handset to the rest of the telephone by low-power radio waves. The latest cordless telephones continually monitor several different radio communications channels and automatically switch to the one that offers the best signal quality. Mobile telephones and pagers communicate by radio waves through a network of local radio transmitters and receivers (see page 12). More advanced mobile

History links

BEFORE TELEPHONES

Long before the telephone was invented, the telegraph provided long-distance electrical communication. Early electric telegraphs worked by making needles on a board swing round to point at letters of the alphabet. One telegraph used up to five separate wires. In 1844, Samuel Morse invented a code of short and long electrical pulses – dots and dashes – in order to send messages along a single wire.

A Morse tapper, used to send messages in Morse code

UNDERWATER CABLES

MILLIONS OF TELEPHONE CALLS TRAVEL ALONG CABLES LAID ON THE SEA BED. MANY NEW UNDERWATER CABLES ARE PLANNED FOR THE FUTURE.

When the first transatlantic telephone cable (TAT-1) was laid in 1956, it provided only 36 telephone circuits. Early undersea cables carried information, mostly telephone calls, as electric signals that travelled along thick metal conductors. Electric signals fade in a cable more than about 35 kilometres long, so signal-boosting devices called repeaters had to be fitted to the cable. Today, even in this age of communications satellites, undersea cables are still being laid. However, modern cables contain optical fibres made from the purest glass on Earth. These optical fibres carry information in the form of laser beams, and they don't need repeaters. The first fibre optic submarine cable, TAT-8, was laid between the United States, Britain and France in 1988. It could handle 37,500 simultaneous telephone calls.

The latest repeaterless fibre optic cables have a huge capacity compared to the first undersea cables. In 1996, the fibre optic cable TPC-5 (the fifth transpacific cable) was laid between North America and Japan. It can carry more than one million simultaneous telephone calls.

Telecommunications cable is loaded into the hold of a cable-laying ship (top). The cable-laying equipment is prepared (above). The cable disappears under the waves at 14 km/h (above right) and reaches its final resting place on the sea floor (far right).

DIGGING TRENCHES

In relatively shallow waters, communications cables are buried under the sea bed to protect them from damage from fishing nets and ship's anchors. The trench-digging and cable-burying work is done by unmanned underwater vehicles. TPC-4 was buried by Sea Plow VII, an underwater robot capable of working down to a depth of 1400 metres.

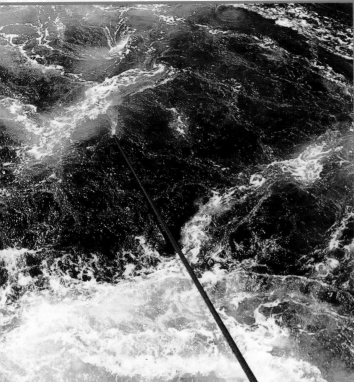

21ST-CENTURY CABLES

Even as TPC-5 was being laid across the Pacific Ocean, plans were being made for the next transpacific cable. TPC-6 will form part of a larger cable system between Japan and the USA. It will have an enormous capacity compared to earlier undersea cables. Initially it will be able to carry one million simultaneous telephone calls, but its capacity will be capable of being expanded to carry 7.7 million calls at the same time. Two thirds of the Earth's circumference is now spanned by optical fibres. At 28,000 kilometres, the Fibre-optic Link Around the Globe (FLAG), is the longest man-made structure ever assembled.

History links

THE EARLIEST UNDERSEA CABLES

The first underwater communications cable was laid between Britain and France in 1851 to carry telegraph signals. The first transatlantic telegraph cable was laid in 1858, after two unsuccessful attempts, but this cable failed after two months. A successful transatlantic telegraph service finally opened in 1866.

RELAYS IN SPACE

AT 36,000 KILOMETRES ABOVE THE EQUATOR, A NECKLACE OF COMMUNICATIONS SATELLITES (COMSATS) CIRCLES THE EARTH, SILENTLY RELAYING TELEPHONE CALLS, TELEVISION PROGRAMMES AND COMPUTER DATA FROM ONE SIDE OF THE WORLD TO THE OTHER.

An Intelsat VI communications satellite is silhouetted against the Earth. This picture was taken from the Space Shuttle Endeavour in 1990.

Radio transmitters need to be placed high above the ground so that their signals are not blocked by tall buildings or hills. The higher the transmitter, the further its signals can travel. A satellite far out in space can see half the Earth. It works like a transmitter on top of a very tall tower. Radio signals are beamed up to it from Earth and re-transmitted down to a different part of the globe. It would require hundreds of transmitters on the ground to do the same job.

Satellites provide reliable, good-quality communications to people anywhere in the world. Using a satellite telephone, people in remote areas can make a telephone call as easily as they can in the middle of a city. Satellite telephones are so small that explorers and people working in distant parts of the world can carry one in a backpack. Roving news-gathering teams can pack one in their car along with their cameras and sound equipment. Satellites are also used to pick up radio distress signals from ships and yachts in difficulty, so that search and rescue services can find them.

CHOOSING AN ORBIT

A satellite's speed in orbit depends on how far away it is from the Earth. A satellite close to the Earth has to race around every 90 minutes or so to resist the pull of the Earth's gravity. A satellite further away, where gravity is weaker, can orbit more slowly. At a distance of 36,000 kilometres, the satellite makes one orbit in the same time as it takes the Earth to turn once on its axis – 24 hours. This special orbit is called geostationary orbit. The advantage of placing a satellite in geostationary orbit is that it stays in the same place in the sky. Dish aerials on Earth don't have to swivel constantly to follow it across the sky.

However, the distance of a satellite from Earth can also be a disadvantage. If your telephone call is connected by satellite, your voice has to travel up to the satellite and back to Earth. Then the other person's voice has to make the return journey before you hear anything.

That's a total of 144,000 kilometres. Even though radio signals travel at the speed of light (300,000 kilometres per second) the journey takes about half a second, or double that if two satellites are involved. This time delay can make it difficult to carry on a conversation.

THE COMSAT BUSINESS

Although most satellites are launched or operated by government agencies, scientific bodies or military organisations, most communications satellites are launched by private companies who offer communications services for sale. Intelsat and Inmarsat are two of the longest established satellite communications organisations. Intelsat has a fleet of 19 satellites in geostationary orbit, with half a dozen new satellites due for launch in the near future. Inmarsat's fleet of nine satellites provides mobile communications to people on the land, at sea and in the air.

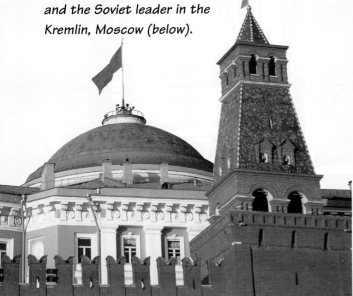

In 1974, Intelsat opened a direct satellite link, or 'Hot Line', between the US president in the White House, Washington DC (above), and the Soviet leader in the Kremlin, Moscow (below).

History links

HOW IT ALL STARTED

In 1945, Arthur C. Clarke (below, at his home in Sri Lanka) invented the idea of the geostationary communications satellite in an article written for *Wireless World* magazine. He showed that three satellites spaced out equally around the world in geostationary orbit could relay telephone calls and other signals between any two points on Earth.

MOBILE TELEPHONES

MOBILE TELEPHONES COMMUNICATE BY MEANS OF HUNDREDS OF RADIO AERIALS DOTTED ALL OVER THE COUNTRY. THE NEXT GENERATION OF MOBILE TELEPHONES WILL DISPENSE WITH THESE AERIALS BY USING SWARMS OF SATELLITES IN ORBIT AROUND THE EARTH.

Mobile phone

Mobile telephones are used by millions of people in all walks of life. A mobile telephone is a miniature radio transmitter and receiver. It works by sending out radio waves to nearby aerials. Each aerial serves all the mobile telephones in a small area called a cell. If a caller moves from one cell to another, the call is automatically switched to the aerial in the next cell. The aerials are connected to exchanges which are linked to the public telephone network. However, there are large parts of the world where there are no mobile telephone aerials and where these mobile telephones cannot be used. The answer to this problem for new mobile phone networks is to use satellites in space instead of aerials on the ground.

Base station

A mobile phone communicates by radio with its nearest radio base station aerial. This message is relayed to a mobile telephone network exchange, which then connects the call to the public switched telephone network (PSTN). This is the network to which all fixed telephones are also linked.

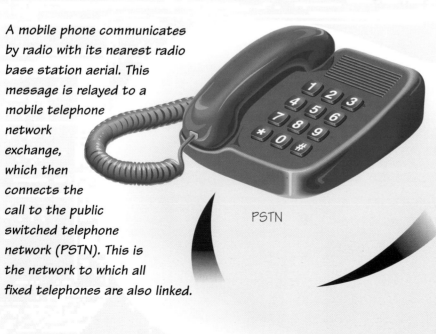

PSTN

Mobile phone exchange

TOMORROW'S MOBILES

Mobile telephones cannot use existing communications satellites. This is because the satellites orbit too far away from Earth for the tiny radio transmitter in a mobile telephone to reach them. The transmitter in the telephone can't be made more powerful because of the possibility of health problems caused by holding a powerful radio transmitter so close to the head.

In the near future, mobile telephones will use satellites that orbit much closer to the Earth than existing communications satellites. The reduced distance between these satellites and Earth means that the radio transmitter in a mobile telephone will be powerful enough to reach them. One advantage of this system is that the calls relayed by lower satellites will travel a shorter distance, and the time delay in conversations will be shorter (see page 11).

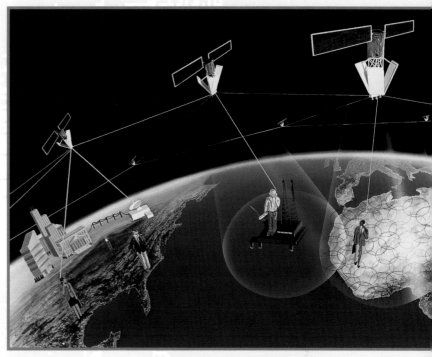

One of the new generation of satellite communications systems for mobile telephones, Motorola's Iridium network, is already using a fleet of 66 satellites flying from pole to pole.

BEWARE THE BELTS

The altitude (height) of a low-orbit satellite has to be chosen carefully. There are two belts of electrically charged particles, called the Van Allen radiation belts, trapped in the Earth's magnetic field. The inner and more intense of the two belts sits between 1000 and 5000 kilometres above the equator. So, low-flying satellites have to orbit at a height of less than 1000 kilometres or more than 5000 kilometres to avoid this belt of damaging particles.

SWARMS OF SATELLITES?

Existing communications satellites orbit at a height of 36,000 kilometres. At that altitude, telephone calls can be relayed around the world by only three or four satellites. Satellites in lower orbits 'see' less of the Earth and so more of them are needed for global coverage. About a dozen satellites are needed at a height of 10,000 kilometres, or more than 50 satellites at a height of only 1000 kilometres.

History links

● ECHOES FROM SPACE
The first communications satellite, Echo, was launched in 1960. Radio signals bounced off it like light off a mirror. In 1962, a new type of comsat was launched. Called Telstar, it received radio signals from Earth and then re-transmitted them down again. Telstar relayed television pictures across the Atlantic Ocean for the first time, but its low orbit meant that it could be 'seen' from both sides of the ocean for only 20 minutes at a time.

SPACECRAFT COMMUNICATIONS

WHEN THEY ARE IN ORBIT, SPACECRAFT COMMUNICATE WITH EARTH VIA A NETWORK OF COMMUNICATIONS SATELLITES AND GROUND STATIONS. THE SPACE NETWORK OF THE US SPACE AGENCY, NASA, TRACKS BOTH SATELLITES AND SPACECRAFT, RELAYING RADIO SIGNALS BETWEEN THEM, AND TO CONTROLLERS ON EARTH.

Satellites in low orbits around Earth rise and set in the sky like the Sun. If a radio dish on Earth is to keep in touch with one of these satellites, it has to swivel constantly and precisely to follow the satellite's flight path across the sky. Polar satellites, which orbit from pole to pole, also have to be tracked. But since the 1980s, NASA has been able to communicate with any low-orbit satellite or other spacecraft, such as the Space Shuttle, without having to follow their movements directly. A fleet of special communications satellites called Tracking and Data Relay Satellites (TDRS) are the key to this new system.

NASA has two networks that work together to provide two-way communications with satellites and spacecraft in low orbit around the Earth. They are the Space Network and the Ground Network. The Space Network is made up of six Tracking and Data Relay Satellites (TDRS) in geostationary orbit which hover 36,000 kilometres above the Earth's equator. The Ground Network is a series of Earth stations equipped with radio dishes that send radio signals up to the TDRS and receive radio signals sent back down from them.

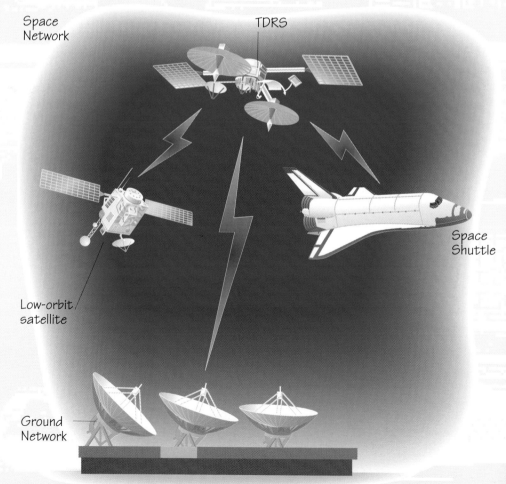

Space Network

TDRS

Space Shuttle

Low-orbit satellite

Ground Network

TDRS

The six TDR satellites track satellites or spacecraft circling the planet beneath them. To communicate with any satellite or spacecraft in a low orbit, a radio dish on Earth is pointed at one of the TDR satellites. The TDR satellite does all the hard work of tracking the low-orbit satellite. The great advantage of the TDRS system is that the ground station dishes do not need to track spacecraft themselves, making the Earth-bound part of the network much simpler and less expensive.

NEXT GENERATION COMSATS

The current TDR satellites have a lifetime of ten years and they will soon need to be replaced. The next fleet of Space Network satellites is already being built. The new design is called the Advanced Tracking and Data Relay Satellite (ATDRS). At 1.6 tonnes, the new satellites are lighter than the craft they are replacing. Their solar panels generate more electrical power, 2300 watts, for the on-board radio equipment. The satellites are also equipped with nickel-hydrogen batteries to supply electricity while they pass through the Earth's shadow.

This new constellation of ATDRS comsats is due to be in orbit above the Pacific and Atlantic oceans by the end of the year 2000. One of their jobs will be to relay radio communications between Earth and the new International Space Station.

A space shuttle orbiter docks with the International Space Station (ISS). Satellites will relay radio communications between the Space Station and Earth.

History links

● NOW YOU SEE IT, NOW YOU DON'T

● When satellite communications began in the 1960s, transatlantic television broadcasts had to be timed to fit into the 20-minute slot when a satellite was above the horizon and in touch with ground stations on both sides of the ocean. The phrase "We have to finish now, because we're about to lose the satellite" was common in those early satellite link-ups.

DEEP SPACE NETWORK

THE US SPACE AGENCY NASA HAS SENT SPACECRAFT FAR INTO THE OUTER REACHES OF THE SOLAR SYSTEM. THE AGENCY KEEPS IN TOUCH WITH ITS DEEP SPACE PROBES 24 HOURS A DAY THROUGH A WORLDWIDE NETWORK OF RADIO DISHES ON EARTH.

Voyager 2 beams data back to Earth as it flies past the planet Neptune in 1989, before leaving the Solar System.

In order to communicate with space probes that venture to the planets, far away from Earth, NASA has a communications network called the Deep Space Network (DSN). This network is specially designed to communicate with distant spacecraft. The Deep Space Network links NASA's command centres on Earth with space probes flying further than 16,000 kilometres from Earth.

The Deep Space Network is made up of three Earth stations. One is at Goldstone in California, the second is near Canberra in Australia, and the third is near Madrid in Spain. These locations were chosen carefully. They are exactly 120 degrees apart – one third of the way round the world from each other. These particular places were selected so that at least one of them is always in line-of-sight contact with a space probe, wherever the probe is in the solar system or beyond. Each Earth station has two 34-metre diameter radio dishes (also called dish antennae), one 26-metre dish and one giant 70-metre dish.

As each station points its dishes at a spacecraft it transmits commands to it from NASA's Jet Propulsion Laboratory (JPL) in California, USA. Data received from a spacecraft is processed at the station and then relayed to the Jet Propulsion Laboratory. It undergoes further processing at JPL before being sent out to science teams who analyse and interpret it.

Radio dishes grow old and eventually they are 'retired'. One of the oldest Deep Space Network dish antennae at Goldstone, called DSS 12, has now been retired from the Network and converted into a radio telescope for school children all over the United States to use.

TWO DISHES ARE BETTER THAN ONE?

Radio dishes can be linked together so that they behave like one larger dish. This technique is called arraying. When radio telescopes are arrayed, they can produce more detailed radio images. The Deep Space Network dishes can be arrayed too. Two 34-metre dishes linked together perform like a 70-metre dish. So, if the station's only 70-metre dish has to be taken out of service for any reason, the smaller dishes can take its place with no loss in performance.

The Mars Pathfinder probe (below) examined rocks and dust on the planet Mars in 1997 and sent information back to Earth via the Deep Space Network.

MORE AND MORE DISHES

As more space probes are launched to the planets, ever greater demands are being placed on the Deep Space Network. So, more dishes are being added to it. The DSN Antenna Project has provided another five 34-metre dishes – three at Goldstone and one each at Canberra and Madrid. These new dishes are completely different from the older ones. Most dish antennae collect radio energy and focus it on to a receiver held above the centre of the dish. The new dishes carry the focused radio energy down below the dish into an underground room to the electronic equipment housed there. Keeping sensitive electronic equipment underground protects it from the weather and enables changes and repairs to be made more easily.

History links

● ENLARGING THE NETWORK

● The Deep Space Network was set up in the 1960s.

● The original radio dishes were 26 metres across.

● Later, they were enlarged to 34 metres so that they could communicate with the Voyager probes far away in deep space.

GLASS WEBS

A NETWORK OF LIGHT-CARRYING GLASS FIBRES IS SPREADING OUT ACROSS THE WORLD, REPLACING OLDER COPPER CABLES AND ELECTRICITY AS THE WORLD'S INFORMATION CARRIERS. IN TOMORROW'S WORLD, INFORMATION OF ALL SORTS WILL PLY THE EARTH'S INFORMATION TRADE ROUTES AT THE SPEED OF LIGHT.

Optical fibres are made from incredibly pure glass. If a block of optical fibre glass was 20 kilometres thick, it would still be as clear as a window pane.

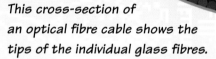

This cross-section of an optical fibre cable shows the tips of the individual glass fibres.

Today, an increasing number of homes are being connected to cable services. These services use just one cable to carry television, radio and telephone signals. Inside the cable are hair-thin glass fibres. Glass cables are replacing copper cables because they are better than copper in almost every way. Light travels along each fibre like water down a pipe, bouncing off the sides instead of escaping through them. You can see the 'light-pipe' effect in a fibre optic lamp or ornament. Coloured lights in the base shine up through a bundle of fibres. The fibres themselves are not very bright because little light escapes through their sides, but the ends of the fibres are a mass of brightly coloured spots of light.

GLASS OR METAL

An optical cable can carry as much information, or as many telephone calls, as a metal cable more than ten times as thick. A fibre as thin as a human hair can carry 17,000 telephone conversations, all going on at the same time. All kinds of information – computer data, telephone calls, video recordings, television programmes, CD-quality sound – can be sent along the same optical cable. Light fades as it travels along an optical cable far less than electric current travelling along a metal cable. Optical cables are also made from less expensive materials than metal cables. Glass is made from sand – one of the cheapest and most plentiful raw materials on Earth – while metal cables are made from much more expensive copper. Metal cables suffer from electrical interference, which has no effect at all on optical fibres. And, finally, optical cables are much more secure than metal cables. It is very difficult for anyone to listen to the messages travelling along an optical cable without cutting it, which is detected instantly.

LASERS FOR COMMUNICATIONS

The idea of laser beams travelling along strands of glass conjures up an image of intense beams of light flickering as they transmit information along a transparent fibre. In fact, the laser beams that whizz back and forth along optical fibres are invisible. Infrared lasers are used, because the glass used to make optical fibres is more transparent to infrared radiation than visible light. This means that an infrared laser beam can travel further along a fibre than a visible-light laser beam.

John Glenn, the first US astronaut to orbit the Earth in 1962, returned to space in 1998, when he joined the crew of Space Shuttle flight STS-95.

G'DAY JOHN!

Of course, it is possible to communicate with light without using optical fibres. Flashing lights were used to send signals between ships during World War II using a device called an Aldis Lamp. The people of Perth, Australia, have used light to communicate with an astronaut in space. When John Glenn made his first spaceflight in his Mercury capsule, in 1962, every available light in Perth was switched on as Glenn's spacecraft passed over the city. When he returned to space in the Space Shuttle in 1998, the people of Perth repeated their gesture of goodwill to the 77-year-old astronaut – who saw it once again.

History links

● **THE FIRST FIBRE LINK**
The optical fibre was invented in 1955 by Indian scientist Professor Narinder S. Kapany. In 1966, scientists in England began working on sending information along optical fibres. The first fibre optic telephone cable was laid between Hitchin and Stevenage in England in 1978. It could carry 2000 telephone calls.

THE INTERNET

THE INTERNET IS A GLOBAL NETWORK OF COMPUTERS HOLDING DATA ABOUT EVERY IMAGINABLE SUBJECT. IT IS ALSO A HIGH-SPEED CHANNEL FOR COMMUNICATIONS, ALLOWING PEOPLE TO SEND ELECTRONIC MESSAGES (EMAIL) TO THE OTHER SIDE OF THE WORLD IN SECONDS.

Logging on in an Internet café. The World Wide Web is a vast store of information that is held in computers all over the world.

You can book a holiday, read a newspaper, visit a library, play games, buy clothes, and do a million other things by looking in the right place on the Internet. Businesses have discovered that the Internet can provide a 24-hour showcase for their products and services, and fast communications with their staff, customers and business partners. Virtual companies and businesses are springing up on the Internet. Some companies have set up paperless office networks. Messages and reports that used to be printed on paper are now created, sent and filed electronically. Internet email is rapidly replacing the fax machine and letter post.

THE WORLD WIDE WEB

The Internet is an interconnected network of computers. The World Wide Web is an extra feature that was added to the Internet later. It allows pages of information held in one computer to include links that take a user directly to related pages of information held in other computers. Clicking on the link – a highlighted word, icon or graphic button – automatically calls up a new web site in a different computer somewhere else. The World Wide Web, which was invented by the British scientist Tim Berners-Lee, makes it easy to move from one web site to another and to find information.

A program called a browser is needed to navigate around the World Wide Web. Programs called search engines also help to find web sites. Keying in a word such as 'astronauts' produces a list of thousands of web sites. Adding more words to the search, such as 'Apollo astronauts' or 'French astronauts', narrows down the search.

WHO OWNS THE INTERNET?

Everyone and no one owns the Internet. Who owns the millions of telephone calls whizzing around the world every day? Once information is let loose on the Internet, no one knows where it will go or how it might be used. Unlike newspapers and books, which can be controlled or censored by governments, it is very difficult to regulate the contents of the Internet. This worries some governments, especially those not accustomed to allowing free expression in their countries. The fax machine began the process of allowing people to exchange ideas and information freely. Today, the Internet has caused an explosion of free speech all over the world.

When the British team that set the first supersonic land speed record found that they could not afford the fuel to fly their Thrust SSC car to the United States for the record attempt, news of the problem was posted on the team's Internet web site. Supporters all over the world each bought 25 gallons of fuel at the rate of 30,000 gallons per day until all the fuel had been paid for. It was an impressive demonstration of the power of the Internet.

WRISTWATCH EMAIL

The microchip manufacturer National Semiconductor is designing a sub-processor, a tiny part of a larger microchip, that will allow the chip to link up with and communicate via the Internet. This will mean that any electronic device, from a food mixer or a CD player to a washing machine or a central heating system, could have its own email address. And that means you will be able to communicate with any electronic device in your home from anywhere on Earth! It also means that you could carry your Internet terminal around with you in something as small as your wristwatch mobile telephone.

History links

WHERE DID THE INTERNET COME FROM?

The Internet began as a small network of computers set up by the US government for military research and communications. It was called ARPAnet (Advance Research Projects Agency network). At the same time, universities and other organisations started setting up their own computer networks. Eventually, they were all linked together by telephone to form the Internet. As soon as they were linked to the telephone network, anyone with a computer, a modem and communications software could connect to them, too.

BREAKING THE SPEED LIMIT

ONE OF THE MOST COMMON COMPLAINTS ABOUT THE INTERNET IS THAT IT'S TOO SLOW. TO PUSH MORE INFORMATION FASTER THROUGH THE NETWORK, NET TECHNOLOGISTS ARE COMING UP WITH NEW IDEAS TO BREAK THE SPEED BARRIER AND UNLEASH THE POWER OF THE INTERNET.

Most personal computers access the Internet by using a modem to connect them to a telephone line. Modems are slow, but faster connection methods are coming soon.

Most Internet users get online by using a modem to link their computer to a telephone line. The modem changes computer data into tones that travel down a telephone line in the same way as a caller's voice. However, data can travel through the network to and from your computer only as fast as the slowest link in the communications chain – the telephone connection in your home.

THE SPEED LIMIT

Telephones and telephone lines were originally designed to carry the sound of the human voice. The sound of a voice is a vibration in the air. Telephones take the most important part of the voice – up to about 4000 vibrations per second – and change it into an electric current of 4000 vibrations per second. This electric current is then carried along the telephone line. Although most modern telephone networks use super-fast fibre optic cables, telephones are still designed to handle a maximum of 4000 vibrations per second.

A modem can fit about 64,000 bits of computer data per second into this signal. In practice, even the fastest modems rarely work faster than about 50,000 bits per second. This is fast enough for small amounts of text, still pictures and slow, jerky video snips, but far too slow for the high-quality video or television pictures that many people would like to be able to send and receive.

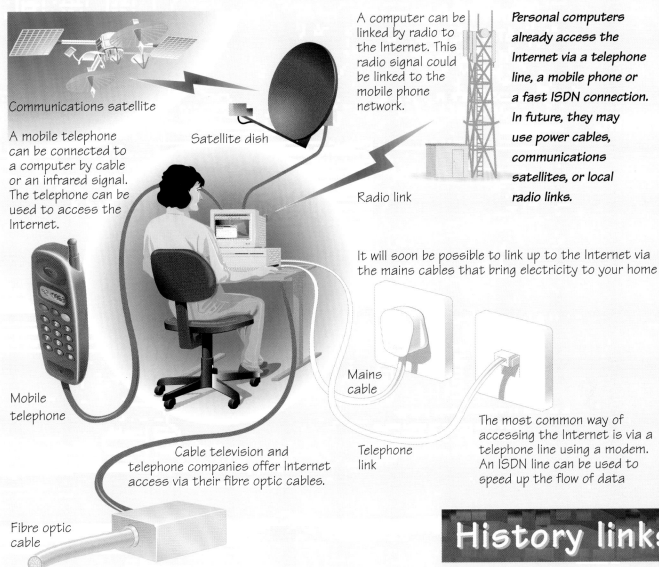

Communications satellite

A computer can be linked by radio to the Internet. This radio signal could be linked to the mobile phone network.

Personal computers already access the Internet via a telephone line, a mobile phone or a fast ISDN connection. In future, they may use power cables, communications satellites, or local radio links.

A mobile telephone can be connected to a computer by cable or an infrared signal. The telephone can be used to access the Internet.

Satellite dish

Radio link

It will soon be possible to link up to the Internet via the mains cables that bring electricity to your home

Mobile telephone

Mains cable

The most common way of accessing the Internet is via a telephone line using a modem. An ISDN line can be used to speed up the flow of data

Telephone link

Cable television and telephone companies offer Internet access via their fibre optic cables.

Fibre optic cable

BURSTING THE BOTTLENECK

There are ways round this information bottleneck. Businesses often link up to a faster ISDN (Integrated Services Digital Network) line instead of a normal phone line. An ISDN connection can work at 144,000 bits per second, but ISDN is too expensive for most people to use at home. Cable TV companies offer fast Internet access through high-speed modems connected to the same fibre optic cables that bring TV, radio and telephone services into the home. Power companies have experimented with Internet link-ups that bypass the slowest part of the telephone network altogether. Instead of using telephone lines or fibre optic cables, they send computer data down the power cables that bring electricity into the home. The next speed-boosting development, already taking shape in the United States, uses a swarm of low-flying satellites to beam data straight into your computer from space. This system will work thousands of times faster than today's modems.

History links

● SOUND CUPS
The first telephone connections between home computers were made using acoustic couplers. The acoustic coupler was a box with two rubber cups on top which was plugged into the home computer. The telephone handset was pushed into the coupler's rubber cups. A microphone in one cup picked up the bleeping sounds of data arriving through the telephone's earpiece, while a loudspeaker inside the other cup changed the computer data into bleeps to be picked up by the telephone mouthpiece.

SOUND RECORDING

SOUND RECORDINGS CARRY PEOPLE'S VOICES AND IDEAS AROUND THE WORLD JUST AS EFFECTIVELY AS ANY TELECOMMUNICATIONS SYSTEM. RECORDINGS ALLOW US TO HEAR THE VOICES OF PEOPLE WE COULD NEVER HOPE TO MEET. THEY ALSO CHEAT TIME BY LETTING US LISTEN TO THE VOICES OF PEOPLE WHO ARE NO LONGER ALIVE.

Sound recording is the audio equivalent of a book or newspaper – it enables a songwriter's lyrics, a poet's words, a singer's performance or a politician's speech to be communicated to people all over the world. A tape recording can be made, relayed to a studio and transmitted to millions of people within minutes, or it can lie unused for decades before eventually being played. There are two ways of recording sound: analogue and digital. All early recordings were made by creating a copy, or analogue, of the sound. An analogue recording might be a wavy groove in a wax cylinder or vinyl disc, or a magnetic pattern on a strip of plastic tape wound around a reel in a cassette.

SNAP, CRACKLE, POP, HISS!

The machine that plays a vinyl record or an analogue tape can't tell the difference between damage to the record or tape and the recording itself. A scratch in a record and a crumple in a piece of tape are turned into sound along with the recording. And without special sound processing, the hissing noise produced by some magnetic tapes is played along with the recording. The answer is to record sound in an entirely different way – digitally.

With a personal stereo, you can listen to music anywhere. The player is only a little bigger than the tapes it plays. Some personal stereos have a built-in radio, too.

TWO BY TWO

A digital recorder changes sounds into a code, a stream of electrical pulses. As the sound passes through the recorder, it is sliced up thousands of times a second and each slice is changed into a number. This is called sampling.

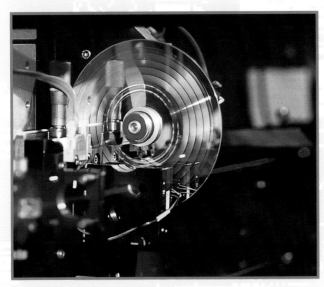

A laser switches on and off at incredible speed as a plastic disc spins, creating a master compact disc from which thousands of CD copies can be made.

In everyday life, we usually count in tens (the decimal system), but it is also possible to count in twos by using only the numbers zero and one. A one might be represented by a magnetised patch on a tape, or a silvery reflective patch on a CD. A zero might be represented by no magnetism on the tape or a dark pit etched into the CD. This is the code used for digital recording. When a tape or disc is played, it is this code that is used to recreate the music. Minor scratches in the disc or background hiss from the tape are not part of the code and so they are not changed into sound.

COUNTERFEIT RECORDINGS

Digital recordings can be copied again and again and transmitted over long distances without any loss of sound quality. This is a great advantage for the recording industry, but it also creates a serious problem. Anyone can copy a digital recording and the copy can be sent anywhere in the world electronically. Although it is easy to copy recordings, it is usually illegal to do so. Recordings are owned by someone and they are protected by the laws of copyright. Copying recordings is theft, just the same as stealing CDs or tape cassettes from shops. Nevertheless, the production of illegal, or counterfeit, CDs and tapes is a huge business. Law enforcement officers are constantly searching for counterfeit recordings and trying to trace where they came from. Some counterfeit tapes and CDs are such good copies that they are almost impossible to spot.

History links

EDISON'S PHONOGRAPH

The first sound recordings were made when the American inventor Thomas Edison (below left) wrapped a cylinder in metal foil. As the cylinder turned, a needle rested against it. When Edison shouted into a horn attached to the needle, the needle scratched a wavy groove in the foil. When he turned the cylinder again, the needle vibrated as it moved along the wavy groove and he heard the faint sound of his voice. Edison's recording machine was called a phonograph.

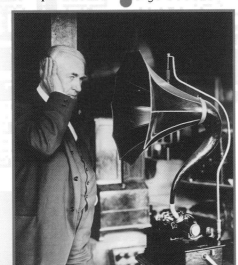

VIRTUAL ARCADES

GAMES ARCADES ARE ABOUT TO BE NETWORKED VIA THE INTERNET. IN THE NEAR FUTURE, YOU WILL BE ABLE TO RACE AROUND A TRACK IN YOUR VIRTUAL RACING CAR, BATTLING ON SCREEN AGAINST ANOTHER CAR WHICH IS BEING DRIVEN BY SOMEONE ELSE HUNDREDS OF KILOMETRES AWAY.

One of the first things people do with any new technology, from the wheel to the internal combustion engine, is to work out how to have fun with it! For example, computers were originally developed to calculate the flight paths of artillery shells and to crack secret wartime codes. They were huge mainframe computers run by teams of specially trained computer operators. It wasn't long before the operators started writing programs to play games at times when the computers weren't being used for anything else. These early spare-time diversions were very simple games, such as noughts and crosses, but, along with the development of the personal computer (PC), they led to the multi-billion-pound computer games industry that exists today.

GAMES ON THE NET

Anything that can be stored in a computer's memory can be sent from one computer to another via the Internet – including computer games. Computer games companies use the Internet to advertise their games. They usually offer visitors to their web sites the chance to download trial versions of their games.

The world's major computer games companies have web sites where players can find game-playing tips and try out new games.

NET-LINKED GAMES

Many of the computer games available today can be played on the Internet with other people around the world. When one games company in the United States launched an online games service, nearly 120,000 people visited the site in its first three weeks. Net-linked games enable players in different cities or even on different continents to play against each other. Huge leaps in the speeds at which data can be transferred between computers via the Internet are expected in the next five to 10 years, so Net-linked games will be able to run faster with more complex graphics and sounds.

The next step, already being discussed by the games industry, is to link games arcades through the Internet. In future,

players or even teams of players in arcades in different places could link up with each other via the Internet to play football or adventure games. They could race in cars, on snowboards or on motorbikes against each other around virtual race tracks, or twist and turn through the sky in Net-linked jet plane fights. The players in different arcades will form a virtual arcade that exists only inside the computers and Internet data links that created it.

People in games arcades on opposite sides of the globe will soon be linked up by the Internet.

History links

● **WHAT A PONG!**
The first computer game was called Computer Space.
● It was invented in 1971 by Nolan Bushnell, who also founded Atari (an international computer games company).
● Computer Space was not very successful but, in 1972, Bushnell produced a game called Pong that became an international bestseller. Pong was a bat and ball game, like electronic table tennis.

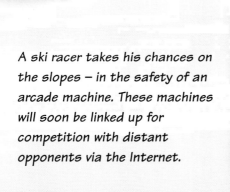

A ski racer takes his chances on the slopes – in the safety of an arcade machine. These machines will soon be linked up for competition with distant opponents via the Internet.

VIRTUAL BUSINESSES

THE INTERNET MAKES IT POSSIBLE FOR A GROUP OF PEOPLE OR COMPANIES IN DIFFERENT PLACES TO WORK TOGETHER AS CLOSELY AS IF THEY WERE IN ONE PLACE. THE INTERNET IS ALREADY CHANGING THE WAYS IN WHICH PEOPLE WORK, AND CREATING MANY NEW POSSIBILITIES.

Laptop computers and mobile telephones mean that 'the office' can now be anywhere, even in a car!

An Internet connection can turn your home or even your car into an office. Letting the information whizz back and forth on the Internet instead of having to go to an office every day is called telecommuting, or teleworking.

TELEWORKING

Now that it has become so easy to move computer data around the world, people with jobs in information-based businesses can work almost anywhere. It no longer makes sense for people to waste several hours every day travelling between their homes and a central office. Writers, designers, accountants and many other people who work with information just need a computer, a telephone and an Internet connection. This makes it easier for people to work from home, and to have more flexible hours so that, for example, they can collect their children from school.

Encouraging more people to work at home should cut down on traffic jams (above) and air pollution, because workers will make fewer car journeys.

Local teleworking offices, or telecentres, are another innovation. People travel a short distance to their nearest community office and use the equipment and Internet connections available there. The office space and equipment are hired per hour or per day – for just as long as each worker needs to use them.

THE MOBILE OFFICE

All the equipment that used to fill an office can now be carried in one small bag – a laptop computer, a mobile telephone and a portable printer (which can double as a photocopier). You can now buy portable colour inkjet printers that aren't much bigger than a paperback book. These printers can also work 'back to front' and scan documents into the computer.

FOLLOW THE SUN

The Internet enables international corporations and virtual businesses to operate 24 hours a day. This is called follow-the-Sun working. The various offices of the business around the world are linked via the Internet. If a particularly difficult problem hasn't been solved by the end of business one day, the problem is entered into a company web site page that can be accessed by any of its offices. As the Earth turns and the Sun rises over the next of the company's offices, staff coming into work look at the page and find any unsolved problems or requests for help that have been left there. They add their comments and suggestions. As the world turns, another office opens and its staff work on the problem, too. By the time the office where the problem originated opens the next morning, the problem has been worked on overnight by staff all round the world. Follow-the-Sun working, using the Internet, multiplies a company's problem-solving power and enables it to work 24 hours a day. It transforms the previously wasted hours of darkness into productive work time.

Link-ups

TELECONFERENCING

People in business often get together for meetings, or conferences. A great deal of time is spent travelling to and from conferences. Teleconferences enable people to stay were they are and meet via a telecommunications link. It's been possible to do this for years, but it needed special studios and communications links. Now, anyone can set up a teleconference using ordinary PCs along with cameras, microphones and software designed to transmit video pictures and voices over the Internet. However, until Internet data speeds increase, the pictures will remain jerky and low-quality.

With a video camera on top, a PC can now double as a video phone, sending voice and pictures via the Internet.

COMPUTER CRIME

THE INVENTION OF THE COMPUTER, ESPECIALLY THE PERSONAL COMPUTER, MADE A NEW TYPE OF CRIME POSSIBLE – COMPUTER CRIME. COMPUTER CRIMINALS STEAL, CHANGE OR DESTROY DATA – SOMETIMES WITH DISASTROUS RESULTS.

There are about one trillion electronic financial transactions every day in the USA alone. In shops, these transactions are checked at the time of the sale. A machine in the shop reads the information stored on the customer's card (above) and communicates with the customer's credit card computer or bank computer.

Today, computer crime is commonplace. The details of someone's bank account, a program that runs a company's accounts, secret information about a new product, the complex set of instructions needed to run a power station – all of these can be stored in a computer's memory. Stealing, changing or destroying any of this data can cause havoc. Someone who breaks into a computer system is called a hacker. One survey in the United States showed that about two thirds of companies and organisations suffer attacks from hackers every year.

CATCHING A VIRUS

A computer virus is a program that spreads from computer to computer, just like an infectious disease spreads from person to person. A virus can infect a computer in two ways – through disks or through networks. People exchange programs and data by giving each other floppy disks and recordable CD-ROMs. If a disk contains a virus, it transfers the virus to any computer system in which it is used. Nowadays, so many computers are linked to networks, such as the Internet, that viruses can also spread easily through the cables and telephone lines that interconnect the network. Once a virus is inside a computer system, it may start working straight away or it may sit there undetected for months. Once triggered, perhaps by a date on the computer's built-in calendar, the virus starts copying itself again and again, overwriting data and programs stored in the computer's memory or hard drive. Most computers are now sold with anti-virus software to scan disks and memory for known viruses. But these programs have to be continually updated, because professional virus sleuths find hundreds of new viruses every month.

CYBER TERRORISM

The economies of the world's major powers are concentrated in 400 cities. These cities are connected to the rest of the world by optical fibres, copper cables, submarine cables, radio-links and communications satellites. It is possible to imagine a determined group of terrorists targeting the biggest and most important of these cities and bringing the world's economy to a standstill by cutting or jamming their communications links. Reliable communications are so important that the companies who design and install communications highways have to ensure that their systems are as secure as possible from attack.

SOFTWARE PIRACY

All sorts of software, from Hollywood movies to pop music, are copied and sold illegally. This is called software piracy. Computer software is affected by this crime too. Software piracy costs computer software producers billions of pounds, dollars and yen a year. Every pirate program that is sold in place of a genuine program robs the computer software industry of some of the profit that is needed to invest in newer, better products for the future.

History links

● **THE FIRST COMPUTER VIRUS**
The term 'computer virus' was invented by Fred Cohen in 1983. As part of his research into computer security, Cohen was the first known person to write a computer virus.

Secure computer systems and communications links are vital to protect financial centres, such as the New York Stock Exchange.

COMPUTER CRIMESTOPPERS

COMPUTER DATA MUST BE PROTECTED SO THAT COMPUTER CRIMINALS CANNOT GAIN ACCESS TO IT. AT THE SAME TIME, THE PEOPLE WHO USE THE DATA NEED TO BE ABLE TO CALL IT UP QUICKLY AND EASILY.

It is almost impossible to find out how much damage hackers do to information stored in computers, but one estimate sets the cost of repairing damage at US$140 billion per year. The enormous size of this figure shows how important computer security has become.

BUILDING FIREWALLS

Computer systems are often protected by passwords, but hackers are experts at getting through or around passwords. People often unwittingly make it easier for hackers to break into computer systems by choosing obvious passwords. The most secure passwords are words that have nothing to do with the data they protect, because they are the most difficult words to guess.

In the business world, computers are often protected by firewalls. A firewall stops damaging computer programs from spreading from one part of a computer system to another. It is a computer program that stands between the outside world and a company's own computer network. Part of the company's network may be open to anyone, perhaps via the World Wide Web, but more sensitive areas are hidden behind a

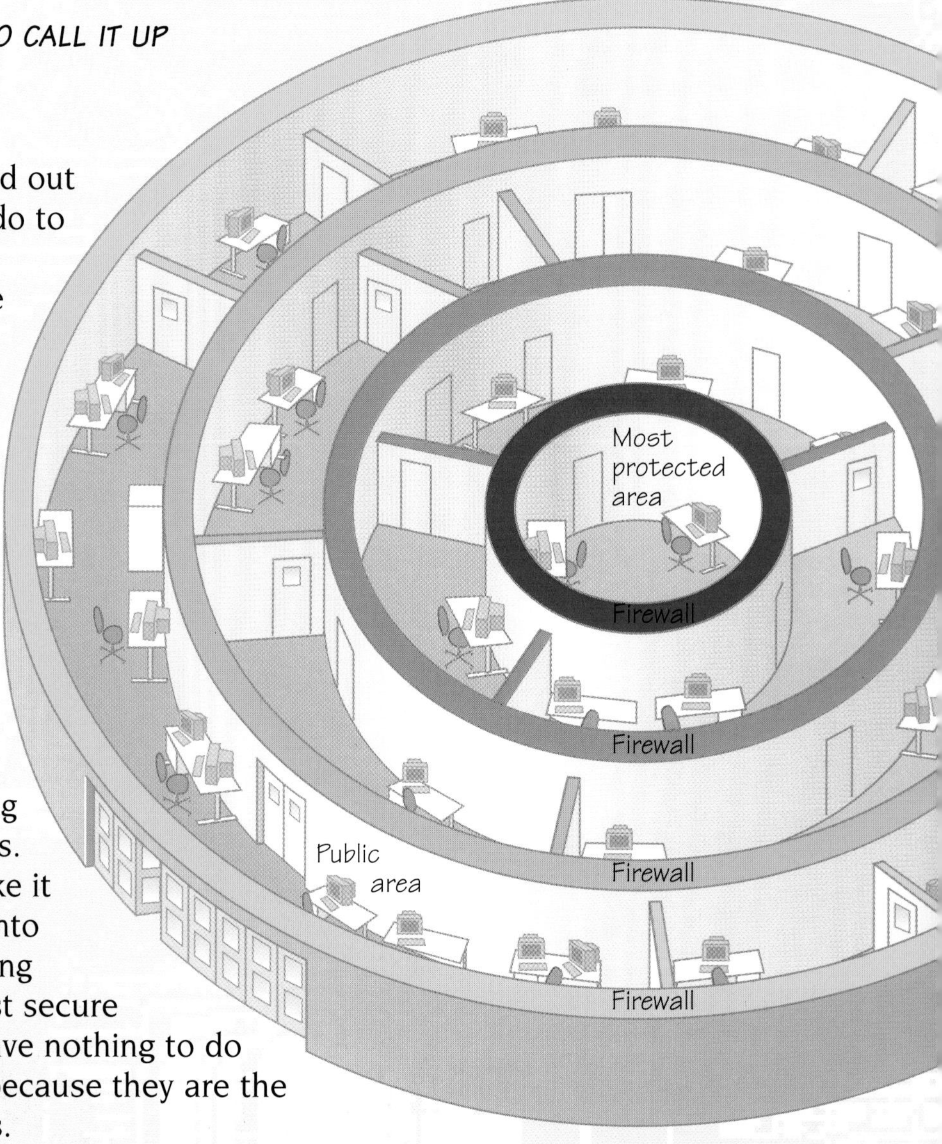

Most protected area

Firewall

Firewall

Public area

Firewall

Firewall

Anyone can enter the public area of a company's computer – the bit that receives post, phone calls, faxes and emails. The firewalls give increasing protection, allowing only certain people access to the most secret part of the network.

firewall. Messages or data that try to enter the secure part of the network are all scanned by the firewall program, which looks for viruses or attempted entry by unauthorised people. A company may have several levels of firewalls protecting more and more sensitive parts of its network, allowing access to fewer and fewer people. However, firewalls are completely useless if floppy disks can be brought in and taken out of the building without passing through security checks.

KEYS AND CODES

One way of keeping communications secure on the Internet is to use secret digital codes. These are much more complex and difficult to crack than passwords. One method attaches a digital code to every message. The code identifies who the message has come from. Only a recipient with the right digital key can unlock the code and read the message. Other security programs work by preventing a downloaded program or email from entering any part of a computer that it could damage, such as the main memory or the hard disk, until a security program has made sure it is safe.

FOILING THE PIRATES

Software piracy is such a serious problem that the world's biggest computer software producers have banded together to form an anti-piracy organisation to combat this crime. In 1998 they succeeded in shutting down Europe's largest-ever counterfeit software operation. Based in Denmark, it had produced 125,000 counterfeit CD-ROMs, containing computer software valued at US$237 million. The CD-ROMs were manufactured in Europe and advertised for sale on the Internet. One team of investigators in Europe is exclusively devoted to tracking down pirate computer software advertised on the Net. They have succeeded in cutting Internet advertisements of pirate software in The Netherlands and Belgium by almost 90 per cent.

History links

CODE-BREAKING

One of the most secret projects of World War II (1939-45) was the construction in England of a programmable electronic computer called Colossus. It was used to decode secret messages sent from the German high command to its military forces, especially its submarines (right). The use of secret codes is called cryptography, which comes from Greek words meaning 'hidden writing'. Changing a message into a secret code is called encoding, or encryption. Changing the code back into a readable message is called decoding, or decryption.

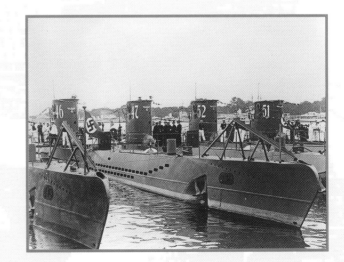

MILITARY COMMUNICATIONS NETWORKS

INFORMATION IS POWER, AND NOWHERE IS THIS TAKEN MORE SERIOUSLY THAN ON THE BATTLEFIELD. HAVING ACCURATE DATA, COMMUNICATING IT TO THE RIGHT PEOPLE AND KEEPING IT SECRET FROM THE ENEMY CAN MAKE AN ATTACK FORCE FAR MORE EFFECTIVE. TOMORROW'S SOLDIERS ARE ALREADY LEARNING HOW TO USE FUTURE BATTLEFIELD INFORMATION SYSTEMS.

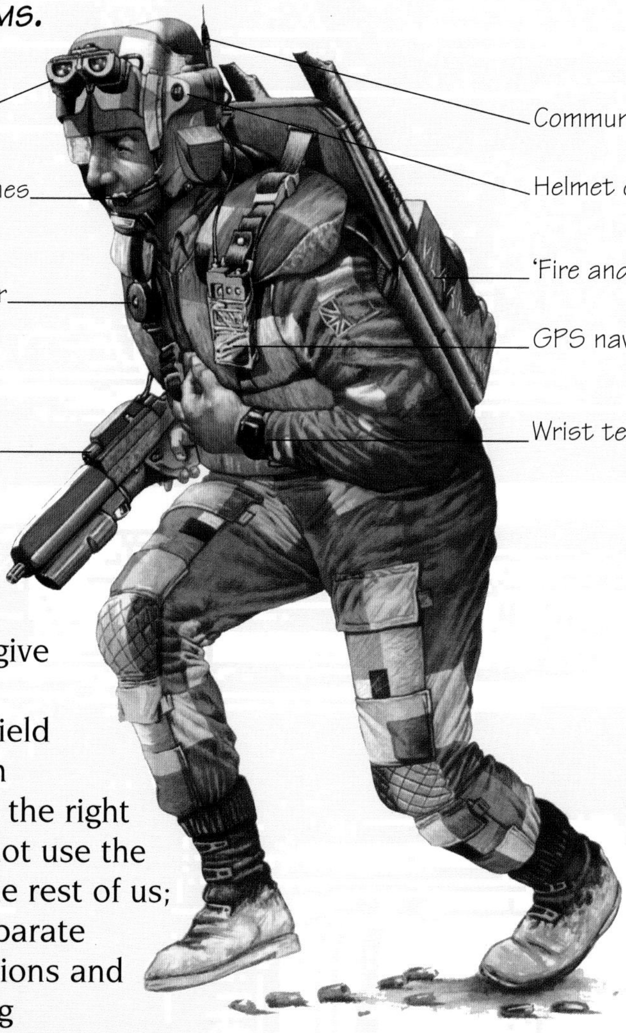

Infrared goggles

Microphone and headphones

Identification transponder

'Smart' personal weapon

Communications radio link

Helmet camera

'Fire and forget' vertical-launch missiles

GPS navigation system

Wrist terminal

Military forces need fast, reliable communications to give politicians, mission planners and battlefield commanders enough information to make the right decisions. They do not use the same networks as the rest of us; instead there are separate military communications and intelligence gathering systems. Dozens of military satellites circle the Earth, relaying coded messages, photographing the ground and searching for heat trails that might mark a missile being launched. A network of underwater microphones, called hydrophones, lies on the sea bed listening for passing submarines.

THE 21ST-CENTURY SOLDIER

In the near future, soldiers will go into battle with helmet-mounted video cameras and palm computers linked to base by radio. Battle commanders will see the images and hear the sounds of a battle unfolding in front of them in real time. Unmanned Aerial Vehicles (UAVs) with video cameras will fly over the battlefield to give commanders a bird's-eye view. Images of the enemy will be relayed via satellite to political leaders, perhaps in another continent, and to troops on the ground. Data will be projected directly on to a head-up screen right in front of a soldier's eyes. The 21st-century battlefield will be awash with information. Victory will very likely go to the fighting force that can analyse and use that information most efficiently.

CYBER SENTRIES

Soldiers standing guard outside military establishments will become an increasingly rare site as cyber sentries take over. Instead of human guards, remote ground sensors (microphones, vibration sensors, infrared cameras and magnetic field detectors) linked by radio to computers will detect intruders much more efficiently than any human. These computerised sentries will release more soldiers for fighting – one soldier can monitor all the sensors in an area that would take 50 human sentries to patrol in the normal way.

SPY DATA FOR ALL?

Some of the photographs taken by spy satellites are now being released to scientists for use in research. Spy satellite photographs are so detailed that sea ice, ocean currents, changes in land use, the destruction of forests, shipping traffic, pollution and many other things of interest to scientists show up clearly. Not every scientist has access to this secret information. The few dozen privileged scientists who have been allowed to see it make up the Medea group. The job of this group is to suggest how the millions of images and thousands of kilometres of computer data tapes might be released and used.

History links

IMPROVED SPY-SIGHT

A series of spy satellites called Keyhole (KH) was launched by the United States from 1960 onwards. KH-2 satellites could photograph objects on the ground that were more than about 12 metres apart. KH-4 satellites could see objects about 1.5 metres apart. By KH-9, the satellite's cameras could see objects about 60 centimetres across. The latest US spy satellites, called Advanced KH-11, can see objects only 15 centimetres across. They relay their images directly to receiving stations on Earth. Earlier satellites dropped film canisters back to Earth.

A network of hydrophones on the sea bed, called SOSUS (SOund SUrveillance System), can detect whales gliding past just as easily as they pick up submarines.

THE NEWS BUSINESS

THE NEWS MEDIA SEND INFORMATION-GATHERING TEAMS TO ALL PARTS OF THE WORLD. THESE TEAMS USE EVERY IMAGINABLE TYPE OF TELECOMMUNICATIONS LINK TO RELAY REPORTS BACK TO THEIR ORGANISATIONS, INCLUDING TELEPHONE, RADIO, THE INTERNET, PORTABLE SATELLITE TERMINALS, VEHICLE-TOP SATELLITE DISHES AND MICROWAVE RADIO LINKS.

In October 1998, a ferocious hurricane swept across Honduras in Central America. Newspaper and TV pictures revealed to the whole world the terrible destruction caused by Hurricane Mitch.

Today, we can turn on our TVs and watch events unfolding almost anywhere on Earth as they happen, or very soon afterwards. Even when an important event is totally unexpected, a natural disaster for example, reporters and television cameras can be on the scene within a couple of hours, transmitting pictures directly to the world's television studios by satellite. Newspapers have to compete with this flood of instant news coverage, so they, too, have streamlined their news-gathering systems using up-to-date technology and high-speed communications.

A worker in a remote region uses a mobile satellite terminal to make a telephone call. The equipment needed to link telephones or TV cameras via satellite is easily transported in a car.

FILMLESS PHOTOGRAPHY

The slowest part of gathering the material for a news story used to be photography. After the photographs were taken, the film had to be developed, dried, printed and the prints dried before the photographs could be scanned into a computer for transmission to the newspaper. Today, when some important photographs are needed urgently, photographers are often sent out with digital cameras. Instead of creating an image on film, these cameras create a digital image that can be downloaded into a portable computer and sent to the newspaper down a telephone line. Within minutes of taking a photograph, it can be in the newspaper's computer system, perhaps on the other side of the world.

ONLINE REPORTERS

In the past, reporters delivered stories to their newspapers by hand or by courier. The invention of the telephone enabled them to phone stories in to fast typists, called copy-takers. Today, newspaper reporters can file (deliver) news stories by means of portable computers. A reporter types the story into a laptop computer and then connects the computer's built-in modem to a phone line. If a telephone line isn't available, the computer can be connected to a mobile phone. At the press of a button, the story is sent straight to the newspaper's computer system within a few seconds.

Link-ups

COPYRIGHT

The copyright laws that protect a writer's work from being copied without permission or payment were passed before CD-ROMs and online publishing became so popular and widespread. Authors have sometimes found their work being used on these new media without their permission and without any payment. Copyright laws have been slow to catch up with the new communications technologies and publishing media.

History links

EAVESDROPPING

In the 1930s, a Polish-born news photographer in the United States called Usher Fellig, nicknamed 'Weegee', had a habit of turning up at the scene of accidents and crimes long before other reporters and photographers. His uncanny skill of getting to the scene first was, in fact, thanks to a radio with which he picked up the Manhattan police and fire departments' radio messages.

PLANE POSITIONS

AIRCRAFT ARE GUIDED AROUND THE GLOBE USING A WORLDWIDE NETWORK OF RADIO BEACONS AND RADAR. INCREASINGLY, AIRCRAFT DEPEND ON SATELLITE TECHNOLOGY TO CALCULATE THEIR POSITIONS.

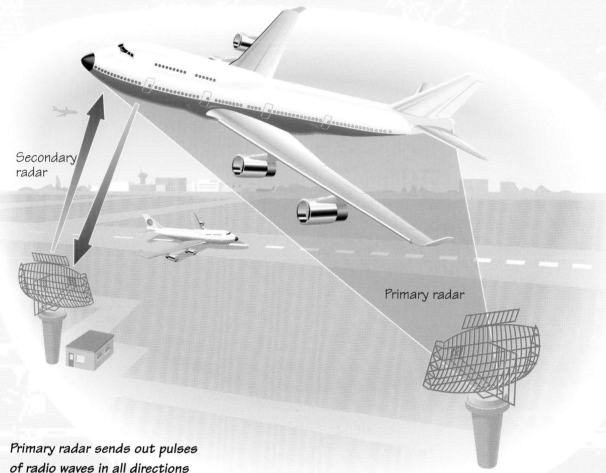

Secondary radar

Primary radar

Primary radar sends out pulses of radio waves in all directions from a spinning aerial. When the waves bounce back from an aircraft, a spot or cross appears on the air traffic controller's screen to show where the aircraft is. When a secondary radar signal is received by an aircraft, the plane sends out a radio message that appears on the air traffic controller's radar screen. This message gives extra information about the plane – its radio call-sign, a code for the airport it is heading for, and its altitude.

Aircraft rarely fly in a straight line from one place to another. Instead, a flight is divided into a series of legs. Each leg usually begins and ends over a radio beacon on the ground. As the plane passes over each beacon, it automatically turns and heads for the next one.

AIR TRAFFIC CONTROL

In most parts of the world, the flight of an aircraft is monitored by air traffic controllers. The controller watches a screen which shows the positions of all the aircraft within a certain area. Two different types of radar work together to produce the map of aircraft positions on the screen – primary and secondary radar.

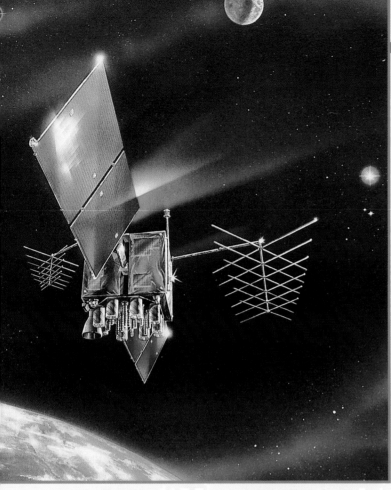

A Navstar Global Positioning System (GPS) satellite circles the world, constantly transmitting radio location signals down to the ground.

SATELLITE NAVIGATION

The Global Positioning System (GPS) is a network of 24 satellites that constantly transmit radio signals. The system was set up by the US Defence Department to enable its soldiers, sailors and pilots to work out their position anywhere on or above the Earth. A small communications terminal containing a radio receiver is used to pick up signals from at least three satellites. It then processes this information to calculate and display its position. Civilians can use GPS too, but random errors are deliberately added to the satellite signals so that the civilian system isn't as accurate as the military system. Russia operates a similar positioning system called GLONASS (the GLObal Navigation Satellite System). The advantage of using satellites, especially for aircraft, is that they give position information over the oceans where there are no radio beacons to navigate by.

PINPOINT LANDING

The Global Positioning System is accurate enough to guide aircraft across the oceans, but it is not sufficiently accurate to be used for automatic landings. An error of a few tens of metres doesn't matter when you are flying more than ten kilometres above the ground, but it could be disastrous if your plane is about to touch down. However, a new system called Differential GPS (DGPS) eliminates the system's deliberate random errors and enables aircraft to work out their position accurately enough for automatic landings.

DGPS relies on the use of a GPS receiver in an accurately known position at an airport. This position is constantly compared to the information given by the satellite signals. The difference between the two is transmitted to the aircraft, and is used to correct the position given by its own GPS receiver. The system is so accurate that it can land the plane automatically.

Existing landing systems guide aircraft by radio beams transmitted from the runway. They force aircraft to make a long, straight landing approach along the radio beams. DGPS will enable aircraft to fly any shape of approach. At least 20 per cent more aircraft will be able to land per hour using this new system.

History links

THE FIRST NAVSAT

The first navigation satellite, Transit 1B, was launched in 1960. It was the earliest of five satellites that formed the first successful global satellite navigation system, the US Transit system, which helped submarines to plot their positions at sea.

WIPE-OUT

SINCE THE SPACE AGE BEGAN IN *1957*, HUMANS HAVE DEVELOPED COMPLEX INTERLINKED COMMUNICATIONS NETWORKS IN SPACE AND ON EARTH. NORMALLY THESE SYSTEMS ARE ROBUST AND RELIABLE, BUT THEY ARE NEVERTHELESS AT RISK OF DAMAGE OR DESTRUCTION FROM THE MOST POWERFUL FORCES IN NATURE.

We all rely on high-speed telecommunications for many of the things we do every day, from making a telephone call or watching satellite television to booking a holiday or using a plastic card to buy something. But there are forces in space and on Earth that are powerful enough to disrupt our communication networks and bring modern life to a shuddering halt.

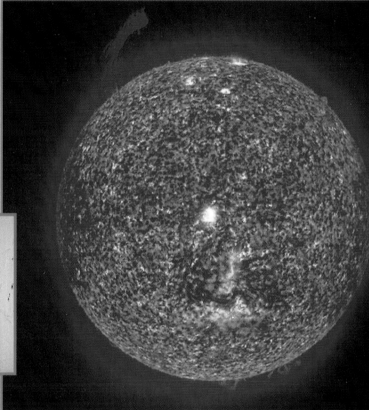

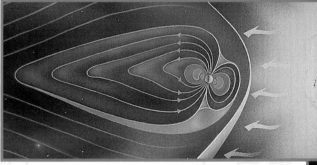

The solar wind (yellow arrows) distorts the Earth's magnetic field (the blue region). Storms on the Sun cause surges in the solar wind that can affect satellites in orbit and cause power blackouts on Earth.

This ultraviolet picture taken by the Solar Heliospheric Observatory (SOHO) shows a solar storm throwing out a huge flare from the Sun.

OUR STORMY STAR

From Earth, the Sun appears to glide silently across the sky each day, a placid and unchanging yellow disc. In fact, the Sun is a boiling cauldron of giant storms and explosions. Solar storms can fling huge clouds of matter out into space. They form shock waves travelling out from the Sun. If a shock wave hits the Earth, it makes the planet's magnetic field wobble, like slapping a big jelly.

As the magnetic field wobbles, it sweeps back and forth across the long cables that carry electricity from power stations to major cities.

When a magnetic field cuts across a wire, it makes an electric current flow along the wire. The current created in a power line by a solar storm can be large enough to trigger safety devices and cut off the power supply. Whole cities can be blacked out.

The electronic circuits in satellites can be damaged in the same way. The shock wave from a solar storm can also push satellites out of position. On March 12, 1989, a shock wave caused by a storm on the Sun hit the Earth. It made satellites in orbit drop a kilometre in height and caused electrical power blackouts across a large area of Canada.

THE COSMIC SHOOTING RANGE

Satellites are also at risk from larger particles of matter flying through space. If you look up into the sky at night, you might be lucky enough to see a shooting star (meteor). This is caused by a piece of dust ploughing into the Earth's atmosphere and burning up. At some times of the year, showers of these particles enter the atmosphere because the Earth has passed through a cloud of dust in space. If any of these particles hits a satellite, it may destroy a vital part of an electronic circuit causing the satellite to break down. Organisations that operate communications satellites often launch an extra satellite to serve as an 'in-orbit spare'. If one of the working satellites breaks down, the in-orbit spare can quickly replace it.

THE NUCLEAR THREAT

Aside from the terrible threat to human life, if there was ever a nuclear war most of the electronic equipment in everyday use would be likely to break down. When a nuclear bomb explodes, it sends out a powerful blast of radio energy called an electromagnetic pulse (EMP). As the electromagnetic pulse sweeps through the circuits of a piece of electronic equipment, it makes electric currents flow in the same way that solar storms cause currents to flow in power lines. The currents produced by a nuclear EM pulse are large enough to destroy the circuits' sensitive electronic components. Unlike the electronic equipment we use at home and work, military electronic equipment is designed to resist EMP.

A nuclear explosion releases a pulse of radio energy powerful enough to wipe out unprotected electronic equipment.

Link-ups

- ### THE MILLENNIUM BUG
  Computers and some other electronic devices have internal calendars. It was feared that equipment which stored only the last two digits of the year might not recognise the year 2000 and the equipment would fail. There were gloomy predictions that equipment ranging from home computers and video recorders to air traffic control systems and power stations could break down as their computers' internal calendars switched to '00'. It was nicknamed the 'Y2K problem' or the 'Millennium Bug'. However, as the year 2000 dawned, there were few reports of any computer problems from either the technically advanced countries that spent most on Y2K solutions, or the less advanced countries that spent the least.

TIMELINE

1753 Scotsman Charles Morrison describes how an electric telegraph might work.

1774 Georges Lesage builds the first electric telegraph.

1783 Joseph and Etienne Montgolfier build the first successful hot-air balloon.

1796 Edward Jenner carries out the first vaccination.

1800 Alessandro Volta invents the battery.

1802 Richard Trevithick invents the steam locomotive.

1844 Samuel Morse invents Morse Code.

1851 The first electric telegraph cable is laid under the English Channel.

1859 Construction of the Suez Canal begins.
The first oil well is drilled in the United States.

1866 The first electric telegraph cable is laid under the Atlantic Ocean.

1876 The telephone is invented by Alexander Graham Bell.

1877 Thomas Edison invents the phonograph sound recorder and player.

1883 The volcanic island Krakatoa explodes, making the loudest bang ever heard on Earth and killing 36,000 people.

1885 Karl Benz builds the first modern petrol-engine motor car.

1888 Emile Berliner invents the recording disc, the 'record'.

1891 Almon Strowger invents the automatic telephone exchange.

1893 Valdemar Poulsen invents magnetic sound recording.

1894 Guglielmo Marconi invents radio communication, also called wireless telegraphy.

1898 Physicist Nikola Tesla shows how to control model ships by radio in Madison Square Garden, New York.

1903 Orville Wright makes the first sustained powered flight.

1909 Louis Blériot makes the first aeroplane flight across the English Channel.
Guglielmo Marconi and Karl Ferdinand Braun win the Nobel Prize for Physics for inventing wireless telegraphy.

1912 The first automatic telephone exchange opens in England.
The passenger liner *Titanic* strikes an iceberg and sinks in the North Atlantic Ocean.

1914-18 World War I.

1926 Robert Goddard launches the first liquid fuel rocket.

1927 Charles Lindbergh makes the first non-stop solo flight across the Atlantic Ocean.

1930 The planet Pluto is discovered by Clyde Tombaugh.
Nylon is invented by Wallace Carruthers at the Du Pont chemical company.
Frank Whittle invents the jet engine.
The tape recorder is invented by the German company I G Farben.

1932 Regular television broadcasts begin.

1935 Radar is invented by a team led by Robert Watson-Watt.

1937 The *Hindenburg* airship crashes to the ground in flames.

GLOBAL NETWORKS DATES

WORLD DATES

1939-45	World War II.
1945	The microwave oven is invented.
1947	Charles 'Chuck' Yeager makes the first supersonic flight in the experimental rocket-plane, the Bell X-1.
1953	Edmund Hillary and Tenzing Norgay climb the world's tallest mountain, Mount Everest, for the first time. The structure of DNA is discovered by James Watson and Francis Crick.
1956	The first transatlantic telephone cable, TAT-1, is laid.
1957	The world's first artificial satellite is launched by the Soviet Union.
1960	The first passive communications satellite, Echo 1, is launched. The first navigational satellite, Transit 1B, is launched.
1961	The first human being to orbit the Earth, cosmonaut Yuri Gagarin, is launched in Vostok 1.
1962	The first active communication satellite, Telstar, is launched.
1965	The first commercial communications satellite, Early Bird (Intelsat 1), is launched.
1967	Christiann Barnard performs the first heart transplant, in South Africa, on Louis Washkansky, who lives for 18 days.
1969	The first human being walks on the moon, Apollo 11 astronaut Neil Armstrong.
1970	The first Jumbo Jet enters service.

1970	The first home video recorders go on sale.
1971	The first Intel microprocessor is introduced. The first space station, Salyut 1, is launched.
1973	Supermarket bar-codes are introduced. The Skylab space station is launched.
1976	The supersonic airliner Concorde enters service.
1977	The science-fiction film *Star Wars* is made by George Lucas.
1978	The first test tube baby, Louise Brown, is born.
1980	The wreck of the passenger liner *Titanic* is discovered.
1981	The US Space Shuttle is launched for the first time.
1986	The Mir space station is launched. The nuclear reactor at Chernobyl explodes.
1987	The world's five billionth person is born.
1988	The first submarine fibre optic telecommunications cable, TAT-8, is laid under the Atlantic Ocean.
1990	Nelson Mandela is released from prison in South Africa.
1991	The first airliners are fitted with satellite telephones.
1994	Nelson Mandela becomes the president of South Africa.
1997	Andy Green sets the first supersonic land speed record in Thrust SSC.

GLOSSARY

ACOUSTIC COUPLER A device used to connect a computer to a telephone line in the early days of computer networks.

ANALOGUE A copy of something in another form – for example, a vibrating electric signal on a telephone line that represents the sound of a caller's voice.

ANTENNA Another name for an aerial. It can be a piece of wire, a metal frame or a dish that is used to receive or transmit radio waves.

BPS The speed of a modem is given in bps, or bits per second. One bit can be either zero or one, the two numbers that make up the binary number system and also computer data.

BROWSER A computer program used for moving from one web site to another on the World Wide Web.

COMPUTER VIRUS A small computer program that invades a computer from a floppy disk or through a telephone connection and destroys data stored in the computer often by copying itself over and over again.

COMSAT Short for communications satellite – a satellite designed to relay communications signals from one place on Earth to another place on Earth.

CRYPTOGRAPHY The science of creating and breaking secret codes.

CYBER A word used to show that something involves a link-up between people and computers using telecommunications. Cyber sentries are computerised guards linked to a central computer system.

DATA Another word for information, especially information stored in, or processed by, a computer.

DIGITAL Made from digits, or numbers. A digital signal carries information as a series of pulses.

DOWNLOAD To copy a program or data into your computer from another computer.

EMAIL Short for electronic mail – mail sent from one computer to another computer by telephone.

ENCRYPTION Converting information or a message into code, especially to keep the information or message secret.

FAQ Frequently Asked Questions. People frequently want to find answers to the same questions, so web sites often have a page entitled FAQ, where the answers to these questions can be found.

FAX Short for facsimile transmission – sending a printed document by telephone using a fax (facsimile transmission) machine.

FIBRE OPTIC The use of optical fibres to transmit light or information.

FIREWALL A computer program designed to protect a computer system from hackers or other unauthorised entry.

FLAG Fibre-optic Link Around the Globe. An optical fibre telephone cable that stretches all the way around the world.

GEOSTATIONARY ORBIT An orbit 36,000 kilometres above the equator. A satellite in this orbit seems to hover over the same place on the Earth's surface.

GLONASS The GLObal NAvigation Satellite System. A Russian navigation satellite network used to locate GLONASS receivers to within a few metres anywhere on Earth.

GPS The Global Positioning System. An American network of navigation satellites used to locate GPS receivers to within a few metres anywhere on Earth.

HACKING Using a computer and a telephone to break into another computer system with the intention of reading, changing or destroying secret information.

INFRARED Invisible electromagnetic radiation that is just beyond the red end of the rainbow spectrum of visible light.

INKJET A type of printer that works by spraying a jet of ink droplets on to paper. A computer controls when and where the ink is sprayed.

INTERNET (NET) A worldwide network of computers linked by telecommunications.

INTRANET A company's internal computer system which is organised like the Internet and accessible using the same software.

ISDN Integrated Services Digital Network. A fast digital connection to the telephone network that can carry voices, computer data and other information much faster than an 'ordinary' telephone connection.

LAPTOP A portable, battery-powered computer designed to be small and light enough to be used anywhere.

LASER An instrument for producing an intense beam of light or other electromagnetic energy such as infrared. Most modern optical communications systems carry information in beams of energy produced by infrared lasers.

MILLENNIUM BUG A problem in the way that computers recognise the year date that many feared would bring some computers to a halt at the beginning of the year 2000.

MODEM A device for changing computer data into tones that can be sent by telephone, and changing received tones back into computer data. The word modem is short for MOdulator-DEModulator.

MORSE CODE A way of sending letters, numbers and symbols over long distances as an electric current or radio signal in the form of a series of short and long tones (dots and dashes).

NASA The National Aeronautics and Space Administration, the USA's space agency, responsible for launching satellites, space probes and the Space Shuttle.

OPTICAL FIBRE A strand of glass designed to carry light for illumination or for communication. A fibre optic cable may contain dozens of optical fibres.

ORBIT The endless path of a satellite circling a planet. An orbit may be circular or the shape of a squashed circle, called an ellipse.

PDA Personal Digital Assistant. A PDA is a mobile telephone that can do more than just make telephone calls. It may be able to send faxes, connect to the Internet and perhaps also work as a personal organiser.

SEARCH ENGINE An electronic index that helps you to find information on the World Wide Web. Using words keyed in by you, a search engine produces a list of web sites that include those words.

SOFTWARE The programs that enable a computer to do something useful. Most software is erased when the computer is switched off. Essential programs that are stored permanently in a computer and are not erased when it is switched off are called firmware.

SUBMARINE CABLE A communications cable that connects two countries by a cable laid on the sea bed.

TELECENTRE A place where people can go to use office equipment and communications services such as the Internet.

TELECOMMUNICATIONS Communications over long distances using telegraph, telephone, cables or broadcasting.

TELECOMMUTING Another name for teleworking – working away from a central office, linked to the office computer system by telecommunications.

TELECONFERENCE A conference between people in different places linked by telecommunications.

TELEGRAPH A system for sending information over long distances by starting and stopping an electric current.

TELEPHONE EXCHANGE A place where telephone calls are switched on to the correct telephone lines.

TELEWORKING Another name for telecommuting – working away from a central office, linked to the office computer system by telecommunications.

VIRTUAL REALITY Pictures or experiences that seem to be real but are in fact created by a computer.

WEB SITE A collection of pages of information located at one address on the World Wide Web

WORLD WIDE WEB A network of millions of interlinked pages of computer data.

INDEX

Internet links

You can find out more about
some of the subjects in this
book by looking at the following
web sites:

http://www.inmarsat.org
(Inmarsat)

http://www.Edu/geography/gcr
aft/notes/gps/gps_f.html
(more information on the Global
Positioning System)

http://passport.arc.nasa.gov/
hst/tour/tdrs.html
(NASA's Tracking and Data
Relay Satellite System
overview)

http://nmsp.gsfc.nasa.gov/
tdrss/tconst.html
(latest information about
TDRSS and Nasa's Space
Network)

http://leonardo.jpl.nasa.gov/
msl/QuickLooks/atdrsQL.
html
(Nasa's Advanced Tracking
Data Relay Satellite System
and satellite details)

http://www.jb.man.ac.uk/
(Nuffield Radio Astronomy
Laboratories at Jodrell Bank,
UK)

http://www.microsoft.com/
games
http://www.activision.com
(internet games sites)